EARNING ONLINE

From Freelancing to Starting a Successful Online Business

Malik Shehzad Khan

KDP

ISBN: 9798389398665
Imprint: Independently published

CONTENTS

EARNING

Earning a living is a necessity for most people, and the traditional way of doing so has been through employment in various industries. However, with the rise of technology and the internet, online earning has become a popular option for many individuals seeking to make a living. Online earning allows people to work from the comfort of their homes, choose their own hours, and have greater control over their work-life balance.

Additionally, the global reach of the internet means that individuals can connect with clients and customers from all around the world. In this way, online earning has opened up new opportunities and has the potential to change the traditional ways of earning a living.

"The Beauty of Earning"

Earning, earning, it's the way

To make your dreams come true each day

A pathway paved with gold and light

To lead you to a life that's bright

Earning, earning, it's the key

To unlock your potential and set you free

To follow your passions, chase your dreams

And make your world burst at the seams

Earning, earning, it's the thrill

Of working hard and seeing the bill

Of reaping the rewards of your labor

And watching your bank account savor

Earning, earning, it's the art

Of turning talent into a smart

And savvy way to make a living

And keep your soul forever giving

Earning, earning, it's the grace

Of taking control of your own race

Of steering your life in the direction

That fills your heart with pure affection

So let us embrace the beauty of earning

And all the possibilities that are churning

Within our souls, waiting to be released

And let us create our lives as a masterpiece.

1. INTRODUCTION

Since the birth of the first man, earning has been a crucial aspect of human survival and development. Earning refers to the process of acquiring income or resources that are essential for meeting one's basic needs and desires. It is an essential aspect of human life as it enables individuals to provide for themselves and their families, obtain basic necessities such as food, shelter, and clothing, and pursue their dreams and ambitions.

Earning has played a critical role in the evolution of human society. Early humans engaged in activities such as hunting, fishing, and gathering to acquire resources needed for survival. As human societies developed and became more complex, individuals engaged in various economic activities such as farming, trade, and craftsmanship to generate income.

In modern times, earning has become even more important due to the complex and interconnected nature of the global economy. With the rise of technology and globalization, the job market has become more competitive, and individuals must constantly acquire new skills and knowledge to remain relevant and employable. Earning allows individuals to invest in their education and training, which, in turn, increases their earning potential and enhances their career prospects.

Earning is also crucial for achieving financial security and stability. By earning a steady income, individuals can save and invest their money, build a nest egg for retirement, and protect themselves and their families against unexpected financial shocks such as job loss or medical emergencies.

Furthermore, earning can also provide a sense of purpose and fulfillment. Many individuals derive a sense of accomplishment and pride from their work and the income they earn. Earning can also provide opportunities for personal and professional growth, as individuals gain new skills and experiences through their work.

In summary, earning is an essential aspect of human life that has played a crucial role in the evolution and development of human societies. It provides individuals with the means to meet their basic needs, pursue their dreams and ambitions, achieve financial security, and derive a sense of purpose and fulfillment from their work.

1.1   Evolution of Earning

Earning has undergone significant evolution over time, from the earliest forms of subsistence activities to the complex and diverse forms of modern economies. This evolution can be traced through the following stages:

Subsistence Economy: This was the earliest stage of earning, where humans engaged in activities such as hunting, gathering, and fishing to meet their basic needs. At this stage, there was no concept of money or trade, and individuals directly consumed or exchanged the products of their labor.

Barter Economy: As human societies became more complex, barter systems emerged, where individuals exchanged goods and services with one another without the use of money. Bartering was used as a means of acquiring goods that were not available locally.

Money Economy: With the emergence of coins and paper money, economies transitioned to a money-based system where goods and services were exchanged using currency. This made trade and commerce more efficient and facilitated the growth of economies.

Industrial Economy: The industrial revolution marked a significant shift in the economy, with the emergence of factories and mass production of goods. This led to the rise of wage labor and salaried jobs, where individuals earned a fixed income for their work.

Service Economy: The service economy emerged in the late 20th century, with the growth of the service sector and the decline of manufacturing jobs. In this economy, individuals earn a living by providing services such as healthcare, education, finance, and entertainment.

Digital Economy: The digital revolution has led to the emergence of a new type of economy, where individuals can earn a living by providing digital products and services, such as software development, online marketing, and content creation. This economy is characterized by remote work, freelance work, and the use of digital platforms for earning.

Earning has evolved from subsistence activities to the modern, diverse economy we have today. The evolution of earning has been driven by technological advancements, changes in the nature of work, and the growth of economies.

1.2   Online Earning

Online earning refers to the process of making money through various online platforms and digital technologies. It involves using the internet to provide goods or services, sell products or merchandise, or generate income from online advertisements or affiliate marketing. Online earning has become increasingly popular with the growth of the internet and the expansion of the digital economy. It provides individuals with the flexibility to work from anywhere, at any time, and can be an excellent source of additional income or even a full-time career.

There are various ways to earn money online, some of which include:

Freelancing: Freelancing involves providing services to clients online. It is a great option for those who have skills such as writing, graphic design, programming, or social media management. Freelancers can work on a project basis or as per their clients' requirements.

Online tutoring: Online tutoring is an excellent option for those who have a teaching background or expertise in a particular subject. It involves teaching students online through various platforms such as Zoom, Skype, or Google Meet.

Affiliate marketing: Affiliate marketing is the process of earning commissions by promoting other people's products or services. It involves promoting products through a website, social media, or email marketing, and earning a commission for every sale made through your referral link.

E-commerce: E-commerce involves selling products or services online through an e-commerce platform. It can be a great way to earn money by selling products such as handmade crafts, digital products, or merchandise.

Online surveys: Online surveys involve participating in market research by sharing your opinions on various topics. Companies pay participants for their time and opinions, making it a great way to earn money in your free time.

Content creation: Content creation involves creating and sharing content such as blogs, videos, or podcasts. It can be a great way to earn money through advertising or sponsored content.

Social media marketing: Social media marketing involves promoting products or services through social media platforms such as Facebook, Instagram, or Twitter. It can be a great way to earn money by managing social media accounts for clients or promoting affiliate products.

1.3   Explanation of the concept of earning online

In today's digital age, there are countless opportunities for individuals to earn money online. This can include providing services to clients, selling products or merchandise, generating income through online advertisements or affiliate marketing, and more.

One of the key advantages of earning online is that it provides individuals with the flexibility to work from anywhere, at any time. This means that individuals can work on their own schedules, and can even work remotely while traveling or living in different parts of the world.

Some of the most popular ways to earn money online include freelancing, online tutoring, affiliate marketing, e-commerce, content creation, and social media marketing. Each of these methods requires different skills and expertise, but they all offer the opportunity to generate income from the comfort of one's own home.

While earning online can be a great way to supplement income or even make a full-time living, it's important to note that it requires hard work and dedication. Success in the digital world often requires building a strong online presence, developing marketing skills, and continually learning and adapting to new technologies and platforms.

Overall, earning online has become an increasingly popular option for those looking to generate income in a flexible and convenient way. With the right skills, dedication, and perseverance, individuals can build successful online careers and create financial freedom for themselves.

1.4   Advantages of earning online

Online earning has become increasingly popular in recent years, as more and more people seek flexible and convenient ways to generate income. There are many advantages to earning money online, from the flexibility to work from anywhere, at any time, to the potential for higher earning potential and job security. Online earning also provides opportunities for personal and professional growth, networking, and skill development. In this article, we will explore in detail the top advantages of online earning and how individuals can leverage these opportunities to achieve financial freedom and career success.

Several other advantages of online earning are as following:

Flexibility: Online earning provides individuals with the flexibility to work from anywhere, at any time, making it an ideal option for those who want to work on their own terms.

Convenience: Online earning eliminates the need for a physical office, commute, and traditional working hours, making it a convenient option for those who want to work from home.

Cost savings: Online earning eliminates many of the expenses associated with a traditional office, including rent, utilities, and commuting costs.

Increased productivity: Online earning can increase productivity as individuals can work in an environment that suits them best, without the distractions of a traditional office.

Global reach: Online earning allows individuals to work with clients or customers from around the world, expanding their reach and potential earnings.

Low overhead costs: Online earning requires minimal overhead costs, making it an affordable option for starting a business.

Multiple income streams: Online earning provides opportunities for individuals to earn income from multiple sources, such as freelancing, affiliate marketing, and e-commerce.

No formal education required: Many online earning opportunities do not require a formal education or degree, making it accessible to individuals with diverse backgrounds and skill sets.

Increased job security: Online earning provides individuals with the opportunity to diversify their income streams, reducing the risk of job loss.

Control over workload: Online earning allows individuals to control their workload, choosing to take on more or fewer projects based on their personal preferences.

Work-life balance: Online earning provides individuals with the opportunity to achieve a better work-life balance, as they can choose to work fewer or more flexible hours.

Higher earning potential: Online earning can provide higher earning potential than traditional jobs, especially for those with specialized skills or in-demand services.

Improved networking opportunities: Online earning can provide opportunities to connect with other professionals and potential clients through social media and online communities.

Skill development: Online earning requires individuals to continually develop and adapt their skills, providing opportunities for personal and professional growth.

Minimal startup costs: Starting an online business often requires minimal startup costs, making it accessible to individuals with limited financial resources.

Access to a global marketplace: Online earning provides access to a global marketplace, allowing individuals to reach customers and clients from around the world.

Reduced environmental impact: Online earning can reduce environmental impact by eliminating the need for a physical office and reducing commuting.

No commuting: Online earning eliminates the need for commuting, saving time and reducing stress.

Increased autonomy: Online earning provides individuals with increased autonomy, allowing them to make decisions about their work and career path.

Improved work satisfaction: Online earning can provide a sense of fulfillment and satisfaction as individuals have the freedom to pursue work that aligns with their passions and interests.

1.5   Overview of the book's content

"Earning Online - From Freelancing to Starting a Successful Online Business" is a comprehensive guidebook that explores the various ways individuals can generate income online. The book covers everything from freelancing to starting an online business and provides practical advice and strategies for achieving financial success in the digital economy.

The book is divided into three main sections. The first section covers the basics of earning online, including an overview of the digital economy, the benefits of online earning, and the various types of online earning opportunities available. This section also provides tips for getting started in online earning, including how to assess your skills and identify potential niches in the market.

The second section of the book focuses on freelancing, providing guidance on how to set up a successful freelance business and how to find and retain clients. This section covers a range of topics, including how to create a portfolio, how to set your rates, and how to effectively market your services online.

The third section of the book focuses on starting a successful online business, providing advice on how to identify a profitable niche, how to create a business plan, and how to build an online presence. This section also covers key topics such as branding, marketing, and customer service.

Throughout the book, the real-world examples of successful online entrepreneurs and freelancers, as well as case studies and exercises are provided to help readers apply the concepts and strategies outlined in the book. Common challenges and pitfalls in online earning are also addressed, such as dealing with difficult clients, managing finances, and avoiding scams.

2. UNDERSTANDING FREELANCING

Freelancing has become an increasingly popular way for individuals to earn income in recent years, offering the flexibility and independence that traditional employment often lacks. Essentially, freelancing involves working on a project or task basis for multiple clients, rather than being employed full-time by a single company. Freelancers have the ability to work from anywhere, at any time, and can often set their own rates and schedule.

However, freelancing also requires a significant amount of self-discipline and self-motivation, as well as the ability to manage multiple projects and clients simultaneously. In this article, we will explore the concept of freelancing in more detail, including the benefits and challenges of this type of work, as well as provide examples of successful freelancers.

2.1   Definition of freelancing

Freelancing is a type of self-employment that involves offering specialized services to clients on a project or task basis, rather than being employed full-time by a single company. Freelancers are independent contractors who work for themselves and have the flexibility to choose their own clients, rates, and work schedule. Freelancers are typically skilled professionals in a specific industry, such as graphic design, writing, programming, or marketing, and they offer their services to individuals or businesses in need of those skills. Freelancers are responsible for managing their own finances, taxes, and client relationships, and they typically work remotely or from their own offices. Freelancing offers the benefits of flexibility and autonomy, but it also requires a high level of self-discipline and self-motivation, as well as the ability to manage multiple clients and projects simultaneously.

2.2   Types of freelancing

There are various types of freelancing work available in the market. Below are some of the most common types of freelancing and their details:

Creative Design Freelancing: Freelancers in this category include graphic designers, web designers, UI/UX designers, and other creative professionals who work with visual content to create designs for websites, logos, branding materials, and more.

Writing and Translation Freelancing: This type of freelancing includes content writers, copywriters, technical writers, and translators who work with the written word to produce high-quality content for various clients. They may work on a wide range of projects, such as blog posts, articles, whitepapers, technical manuals, and more.

Programming and Development Freelancing: Freelancers in this category include web developers, software developers, mobile app developers, and other technical professionals who specialize in programming and development work. They work on projects that involve coding, testing, and debugging software applications.

Marketing and Advertising Freelancing: Freelancers in this category include social media managers, SEO specialists, PPC specialists, content marketers, and other marketing and advertising professionals who work with businesses to create and implement marketing strategies.

Administrative Support Freelancing: Freelancers in this category include virtual assistants, customer service representatives, bookkeepers, and other administrative professionals who provide support to businesses in various areas such as data entry, phone support, bookkeeping, and scheduling.

Consulting and Coaching Freelancing: Freelancers in this category include business consultants, life coaches, career coaches, and other professionals who offer expert advice and guidance to individuals and businesses in various areas such as business strategy, career development, and personal growth.

Audio and Video Production Freelancing: Freelancers in this category include video editors, sound engineers, and other professionals who specialize in producing and editing audio and video content for various clients.

In summary, freelancing offers a wide range of opportunities for professionals with various skills and expertise. Freelancers have the flexibility to choose their clients and projects, set their own rates and work schedules, and work from anywhere in the world. The type of freelancing work one chooses depends on their skills, interests, and market demand.

2.3   Popular freelance platforms

Freelancing platforms have become increasingly popular in recent years, providing a way for individuals to find work and for businesses to find talented freelancers to complete projects. These platforms offer a range of benefits for both freelancers and businesses, including access to a global talent pool, a streamlined hiring process, and secure payment systems. Below are some of the most popular freelancing platforms and their features.

Upwork: Upwork is one of the largest freelancing platforms in the world, with over 12 million freelancers and 5 million clients. The platform offers a range of services, including project management tools, time tracking, and a messaging system. Upwork also offers a wide range of jobs, from short-term projects to long-term contracts.

Freelancer.com: Freelancer.com is another popular platform that offers a wide range of freelance jobs across various industries, including web development, graphic design, writing, and more. The platform offers a bidding system, where freelancers can bid on projects posted by clients. Freelancer.com also offers a range of tools and resources for freelancers, including project management tools and an invoice system.

Fiverr: Fiverr is a platform that offers a range of freelance services starting at $5. The platform has over 3 million active freelancers and offers a wide range of services, including graphic design, writing, programming, and more. Fiverr also offers a messaging system, allowing clients to communicate with freelancers directly.

Toptal: Toptal is a platform that offers access to the top 3% of freelance talent across various industries, including software development, finance, and design. The platform offers a rigorous screening process to ensure that only the best freelancers are accepted. Toptal also offers a range of project management tools and dedicated account managers for clients.

Guru: Guru is a platform that offers a range of freelance services across various industries, including web development, graphic design, and writing. The platform offers a bidding system, allowing freelancers to bid on projects posted by clients. Guru also offers a range of tools and resources for freelancers, including project management tools and an invoicing system.

In conclusion, freelancing platforms have become an increasingly popular way for businesses to find talented freelancers and for individuals to find work. Each platform offers its own unique features and benefits, and it is important to choose the one that best fits your needs as a freelancer or business. With the rise of remote work, freelancing platforms are likely to continue to grow in popularity, providing opportunities for individuals and businesses around the world.

2.4   How to start as a freelancer

Starting as a freelancer can be an exciting and rewarding way to work. However, it can also be challenging, especially if you're not sure where to begin. Below are some steps to help you get started as a freelancer.

2.4.1. Choose your niche: The first step to starting as a freelancer is to decide what kind of work you want to do. This will help you focus your efforts and make it easier to find clients. Consider your skills and interests, and think about what kind of work you enjoy doing.

2.4.2. Build your portfolio: Once you've chosen your niche, it's time to start building your portfolio. A portfolio is a collection of your best work that showcases your skills and experience. You can create a portfolio website or use a platform like Behance or Dribbble to showcase your work.

2.4.3. Set your rates: Before you start looking for clients, you need to set your rates. This can be tricky, as you want to charge enough to make a living but not so much that you price yourself out of the market. Research what other freelancers in your niche are charging and use that as a guide.

2.4.4. Find clients: There are many ways to find clients as a freelancer, including job boards, social media, and word of mouth. Start by reaching out to your network and letting them know that you're available for work. You can also join online communities and forums in your niche to connect with potential clients.

2.4.5. Manage your finances: As a freelancer, you'll be responsible for managing your finances, including invoicing, taxes, and expenses. It's important to set up a system for tracking your income and expenses from the beginning, and to make sure you're saving enough for taxes.

2.4.6. Build your brand: Building your brand as a freelancer is important for standing out in a crowded market. This can include creating a professional website, building a strong social media presence, and developing a unique value proposition that sets you apart from other freelancers.

In conclusion, starting as a freelancer can be a great way to work on your own terms and build a successful career. While it can be challenging at first, by following these steps and staying focused on your goals, you can create a thriving freelance business that provides you with the flexibility and freedom you desire.

2.5   *Tips for succeeding as a freelancer*

As a freelancer, success is not just about finding clients and completing projects. It's also about building a sustainable and fulfilling career that allows you to grow and thrive over time. There are a few tips that can help you succeed in your career of freelancing. Here are some of the most important ones:

Be proactive: As a freelancer, you're responsible for finding your own clients and projects. This means that you need to be proactive and constantly looking for new opportunities. Set aside time each week to network, pitch new clients, and market your services.

Develop a strong work ethic: Freelancing requires discipline and self-motivation. It's important to set realistic goals and deadlines for yourself, and to stay focused on your work even when you don't have a boss or team to hold you accountable.

Communicate effectively: Good communication is essential to freelancing success. Make sure you're clear and concise in your emails and messages, and respond to client inquiries in a timely manner. If there are any issues or conflicts, address them openly and professionally.

Continuously improve your skills: Freelancing is a competitive field, and it's important to stay up-to-date with the latest trends and technologies in your niche. Take courses, attend conferences, and read industry publications to stay on top of your game.

Set clear goals: One of the keys to success as a freelancer is to have clear goals for your career. These might include financial goals, such as a target income level or a certain number of clients, or personal goals, such as improving your skills or building a strong network. By setting specific, measurable goals, you can stay focused and motivated over time.

Manage your time effectively: As a freelancer, time management is crucial. You need to balance your work with your personal life, and you need to be able to meet deadlines and deliver quality work on time. Consider using time-tracking tools, creating a schedule, and setting boundaries to ensure that you're making the most of your time.

Build strong relationships: Building strong relationships with clients, colleagues, and others in your industry is key to long-term success as a freelancer. This means communicating effectively, delivering high-quality work, and being responsive and professional at all times. It also means investing in your network by attending events, participating in online communities, and reaching out to new contacts.

Continuously learn and improve: Freelancing is a constantly evolving industry, and staying up to date with the latest trends and technologies is essential for success. This means investing in your education, taking courses, attending workshops, and staying curious and open-minded. It also means seeking feedback from clients and colleagues and using it to improve your skills and approach.

Take care of yourself: Finally, it's important to take care of yourself as a freelancer. This means managing your stress levels, maintaining a healthy work-life balance, and taking time to recharge and pursue your hobbies and interests. By prioritizing your well-being, you'll be better equipped to handle the ups and downs of freelancing and build a successful and sustainable career over time.

By following these tips, you can set yourself up for success as a freelancer and build a thriving career on your own terms.

3. BUILDING A FREELANCE BUSINESS

Building a freelance business can be an excellent way to turn your skills and passion into a fulfilling and lucrative career. Unlike traditional employment, freelancing offers you the flexibility to work on your own terms, choose your clients and projects, and build a business that reflects your values and goals. However, building a successful freelance business requires more than just technical skills or creativity. It requires a strategic approach to marketing, sales, and client management, as well as a willingness to take risks, learn from failures, and adapt to changing market conditions. In this book, we'll explore the key steps involved in building a freelance business, from defining your niche and brand to finding clients, setting your rates, and growing your business over time. Whether you're just starting out or looking to take your existing freelance business to the next level, here I will provide you with the insights, tools, and resources you need to succeed.

3.1   Establishing a brand

In the world of freelance business, establishing a strong brand is essential for success. Your brand is the way that you present yourself and your services to the world, and it can make a big difference in how clients perceive you, whether they trust you, and whether they want to work with you. In this chapter, we'll explore the key elements of building a strong brand as a freelancer, from defining your unique value proposition to creating a visual identity and developing your online presence.

a. Defining your value proposition

The first step in building your brand as a freelancer is to define your unique value proposition. This means identifying what sets you apart from other freelancers in your field, what specific skills or expertise you bring to the table, and what benefits you offer to clients. To define your value proposition, start by asking yourself some key questions, such as:

-What are my core strengths and skills?

-What problems can I solve for my clients?

-What makes me different from other freelancers in my field?

-What kind of clients am I best suited to work with?

-What values and beliefs do I want to convey through my work?

b. Creating a visual identity

Once you have a clear understanding of your value proposition, the next step is to create a visual identity that reflects your brand. This includes designing a logo, choosing a color palette, and creating a visual style guide that you can use across all of your marketing materials. When creating your visual identity, it's important to keep in mind your target audience and the image that you want to convey. A clean, modern design might work well for a tech-focused freelancer, while a more artistic or colorful style might be better suited for a creative professional.

c. Developing your online presence

In today's digital age, having a strong online presence is essential for building your brand as a freelancer. This means creating a website that showcases your work, skills, and experience, as well as developing a social media presence that allows you to connect with potential clients and showcase your expertise.

When developing your online presence, it's important to keep your brand consistent across all channels, using your visual identity and messaging to create a cohesive and memorable impression.

Conclusion

Establishing a strong brand is one of the most important steps you can take as a freelancer to build a successful and sustainable business. By defining your unique value proposition, creating a visual identity, and developing your online presence, you can set yourself apart from the competition, attract the right clients, and build a reputation for quality and reliability. With these tips and strategies, you'll be well on your way to establishing a strong and recognizable brand that reflects your skills, expertise, and values as a freelancer.

3.2   *Creating a portfolio*

As a freelancer, creating a portfolio is a crucial part of building your brand and establishing your credibility with potential clients. Your portfolio is essentially a collection of your best work, showcasing your skills, expertise, and experience in your chosen field. A strong portfolio can help you stand out from other freelancers and demonstrate your ability to deliver high-quality results.

Here are some key steps to follow when creating a portfolio:

3.2.1. Choose your best work: When selecting pieces to include in your portfolio, focus on showcasing your best and most relevant work. Consider the type of work you want to attract in the future, and choose pieces that demonstrate your skills in that area.

3.2.2. Organize your work: Organize your portfolio in a way that makes sense for your target audience. This could be by project type, industry, or skill set.

You may also want to consider creating separate portfolios for different types of work or clients.

3.2.3. Include project details: When presenting your work in your portfolio, be sure to include relevant project details such as the client, the project goals, and any challenges or solutions you implemented.

3.2.4. Consider visual design: A well-designed portfolio can make a big difference in how potential clients perceive your work. Consider using high-quality images, clear typography, and a layout that is easy to navigate.

3.2.5. Update regularly: Your portfolio should be an ongoing project, and it's important to keep it up to date with your latest work. Consider revisiting your portfolio every few months and removing older work or pieces that no longer reflect your current skill set.

In addition to creating a portfolio, it's also important to make sure that it is easily accessible to potential clients. This could mean creating a dedicated section on your website, sharing it on social media, or including a link in your email signature.

By following these steps and creating a strong portfolio, you can demonstrate your expertise and build trust with potential clients, setting yourself up for success as a freelancer.

3.3   Setting prices and rates

Setting prices and rates is an essential aspect of building a successful freelance business. Pricing your services too high can drive away potential clients, while pricing them too low can undervalue your work and leave you struggling to make ends meet. Here are some tips for setting prices and rates as a freelancer:

3.3.1. Research the market: Before setting your rates, research the going rates for similar services in your industry and location. This can help you get a sense of what your potential clients are willing to pay and ensure that your rates are competitive.

3.3.2. Consider your experience and expertise: Your rates should reflect your level of experience and expertise in your field. If you have a strong track record of delivering high-quality work and have specialized skills, you may be able to charge higher rates than someone just starting out.

3.3.3. Calculate your costs: It's important to understand your costs as a freelancer, including expenses such as software, equipment, and overhead. Consider these costs when setting your rates to ensure that you are earning enough to cover your expenses and make a profit.

3.3.4. Determine your value proposition: What sets you apart from other freelancers? Consider your unique skills and experience, and use this to determine your value proposition. This can help you justify higher rates and attract clients who are willing to pay for your specialized services.

3.3.5. Be flexible: As you gain experience and build your portfolio, you may need to adjust your rates to reflect your changing skills and expertise. Be open to reevaluating your pricing strategy on a regular basis to ensure that you are staying competitive in the market.

Remember, setting your rates is not a one-time decision. It's important to regularly evaluate and adjust your pricing strategy to reflect changes in the market and your own skills and experience. By taking a thoughtful and strategic approach to setting your rates, you can build a successful freelance business that meets your financial goals and helps you achieve professional success.

3.4 Finding clients

Finding clients is a critical aspect of building a successful freelance business. Without clients, you won't be able to earn a living as a freelancer. Here are some tips for finding clients:

3.4.1. Build a strong online presence: Having a strong online presence can help you attract clients who are searching for your services. This includes creating a professional website, setting up social media profiles, and creating a portfolio of your work.

3.4.2. Leverage your network: Reach out to your personal and professional network and let them know that you're available for freelance work. You never know who might be in need of your services or who might know someone who is.

3.4.3. Attend networking events: Attend local networking events and industry conferences to meet potential clients and make connections with other professionals in your field.

3.4.4. Utilize freelance platforms: Freelance platforms such as Upwork, Freelancer, and Fiverr can be a great way to find clients and build your reputation as a freelancer. These platforms allow you to bid on projects and showcase your skills to potential clients.

3.4.5. Cold outreach: If you have a specific client or company in mind that you would like to work with, consider reaching out to them directly to pitch your services. This can be a more time-consuming approach, but it can also be highly effective if done correctly.

Remember, building a client base takes time and effort. Be patient and persistent in your efforts to find clients, and always deliver high-quality work that will help you build a strong reputation as a freelancer.

3.5 Managing projects and delivering quality work

As a freelancer, managing projects and delivering quality work are crucial for building a successful business and maintaining a good reputation with clients. Here are some tips for managing projects and delivering quality work:

3.5.1. Set clear expectations and deadlines: Before starting a project, make sure you and your client are on the same page about the scope, timeline, and deliverables. This will help prevent misunderstandings and ensure that everyone is working towards the same goals.

3.5.2. Create a project plan: Create a detailed project plan that outlines the steps involved in completing the project, including deadlines and milestones. This will help you stay organized and ensure that you stay on track.

3.5.3. Communicate regularly: Communication is key when working with clients. Keep them updated on your progress and ask for feedback throughout the project. This will help ensure that you're meeting their expectations and that the final product meets their needs.

3.5.4. Use project management tools: There are many project management tools available that can help you stay organized and manage your projects more efficiently. Some popular tools include Trello, Asana, and Basecamp.

3.5.5. Deliver quality work: Delivering high-quality work is essential for building a good reputation as a freelancer. Make sure you understand your client's expectations and deliver work that meets or exceeds those expectations.

3.5.6. Review your work: Take the time to review your work before submitting it to your client. This will help ensure that there are no errors or mistakes and that the final product is of the highest quality.

By following these tips, you can effectively manage projects and deliver quality work as a freelancer, which will help you build a successful business and maintain long-term relationships with your clients.

3.6   *Maintaining long-term relationships with clients*

Maintaining long-term relationships with clients is a critical aspect of building a successful freelance business. Here are some tips for maintaining long-term relationships with clients:

3.6.1. Provide excellent customer service: The key to building long-term relationships with clients is providing excellent customer service. Respond to their inquiries and concerns promptly and professionally, and make sure they feel valued and appreciated.

3.6.2. Deliver high-quality work: Delivering high-quality work is essential for building long-term relationships with clients. Consistently meeting or exceeding their expectations will help build trust and confidence in your abilities.

3.6.3. Be proactive: Be proactive in your communication with clients. Don't wait for them to contact you with questions or concerns. Reach out to them regularly to check in and see how things are going.

3.6.4. Stay organized: Keep track of all your projects and client communications in one place to stay organized and avoid missing important deadlines or details.

3.6.5. Ask for feedback: Ask clients for feedback on your work and their experience working with you. This will show that you value their opinion and are committed to improving your services.

Remember, maintaining long-term relationships with clients is essential for building a successful freelance business. By providing excellent customer service, delivering high-quality work, being proactive in your communication, staying organized, and asking for feedback, you can build trust and loyalty with your clients and establish a strong reputation as a reliable and skilled freelancer.

4. EXPLORING ONLINE BUSINESS OPPORTUNITIES

The internet has opened up a world of opportunities for entrepreneurs and business owners. With the rise of e-commerce, digital marketing, and online education, there has never been a better time to explore online business opportunities. Whether you are looking to start a new venture or expand your existing business, the internet offers a wealth of possibilities. However, with so many options available, it can be overwhelming to know where to start. In this section, we will explore some tips and strategies for identifying and pursuing online business opportunities. By following these guidelines, you can increase your chances of success and build a profitable online business.

Exploring online business opportunities can be an exciting and rewarding venture. With the rise of the internet and advancements in technology, there are more opportunities than ever to start an online business. Here are some tips for exploring online business opportunities:

i. Identify a need

Look for gaps in the market and identify areas where there is a need for a new product or service. This can help you create a unique business idea that sets you apart from the competition.

ii. Research your market

Conduct market research to determine if there is a demand for your product or service, and to identify your target audience. This will help you better understand your potential customers and tailor your business strategy accordingly.

iii. Determine your niche

Consider what unique skills or knowledge you possess that can be applied to an online business. Determine your niche and focus on building a business that caters to that specific area.

iv. Create a business plan

Develop a comprehensive business plan that outlines your goals, target market, marketing strategies, and financial projections. This will help you stay organized and focused as you build your online business.

v. Utilize online tools

There are many online tools and resources available to help you build and manage your online business, such as website builders, email marketing platforms, and social media management tools.

vi. Start small

Consider starting with a small-scale project or prototype to test the viability of your business idea before investing significant time and resources into a larger venture.

Remember, building a successful online business takes time, effort, and persistence. Stay focused on your goals, and be open to adapting your strategy as you learn and grow in the world of online business.

4.1   Overview of online business models

Online business models refer to the different ways that businesses can generate revenue and operate on the internet. There are various online business models, each with its own unique advantages and disadvantages. Here is an overview of some popular online business models:

4.1.1. E-commerce: E-commerce refers to businesses that sell products or services online. This can include traditional retail stores that have an online presence, as well as online-only stores that operate exclusively on the internet.

4.1.2. Affiliate marketing: Affiliate marketing involves promoting other businesses' products or services and earning a commission on any resulting sales. This can be a profitable way to generate revenue without having to create and sell your own products.

4.1.3. Subscription-based models: Subscription-based models involve charging customers a recurring fee for access to a product or service. This can include subscription boxes, online courses, or software-as-a-service (SaaS) products.

4.1.4. Advertising-based models: Advertising-based models involve generating revenue by displaying advertisements on your website or social media platforms. This can include pay-per-click advertising, display ads, or sponsored content.

4.1.5. Digital products: Digital products refer to products that can be delivered electronically, such as ebooks, music, or software. This can be a low-overhead way to generate revenue, as there are no physical products to produce or ship.

4.1.6. Service-based models: Service-based models involve offering a service, such as web design, content writing, or virtual assistant services, to clients online.

These are just a few examples of the many online business models that exist. The key is to find a business model that aligns with your skills, interests, and target market, and that offers a sustainable path to revenue generation and growth.

4.2 Popular online business niches

There are several popular online business niches that entrepreneurs can explore. These niches have seen significant growth in recent years and offer unique opportunities for online business owners to establish themselves in a specific market. Here are a few examples:

4.2.1. Health and wellness: The health and wellness industry is a rapidly growing market, with consumers seeking products and services that promote healthy living. Online businesses in this niche can sell health supplements, fitness programs, or provide wellness coaching services.

4.2.2. Personal finance: With increasing financial uncertainty and a desire for financial independence, the personal finance niche has become a popular area for online businesses. Entrepreneurs in this niche can offer financial coaching services, investment advice, or create educational content related to personal finance.

4.2.3. Digital marketing: As businesses shift their focus to online channels, the need for digital marketing services has increased. Online businesses in this niche can provide social media management, content creation, search engine optimization, and other digital marketing services to clients.

4.2.4. E-learning: With the rise of remote work and online education, the e-learning niche has become a lucrative market. Online businesses in this niche can offer online courses, tutorials, or training programs on a variety of topics.

4.2.5. Home improvement: With more people spending time at home, the home improvement niche has seen a surge in demand. Online businesses in this niche can sell DIY home improvement products, provide home renovation services, or offer interior design consultations.

These are just a few examples of popular online business niches. As with any business, it's important to conduct market research and validate your business idea before launching. By finding a profitable niche and delivering high-quality products or services, online entrepreneurs can establish successful businesses that meet the needs of their target audience.

4.3   *Evaluating online business opportunities*

Evaluating online business opportunities is a crucial step in determining whether a business idea is viable and has the potential to succeed. Entrepreneurs need to conduct market research and analyze various factors to determine the feasibility and profitability of their business idea. Here are some important considerations for evaluating online business opportunities:

4.3.1. Market demand: Is there a demand for the product or service that you want to offer? It's essential to determine whether there is a market for your business idea and whether consumers are willing to pay for it.

4.3.2. Competition: Who are your competitors, and how will you differentiate yourself from them? It's important to understand the competitive landscape and identify ways to stand out from the crowd.

4.3.3. Revenue potential: How much revenue can your business generate, and what are the profit margins? You need to analyze the revenue potential of your business idea to determine whether it can generate enough income to sustain itself.

4.3.4. Costs and resources: What are the costs associated with starting and running the business, and what resources will you need? You need to evaluate the costs and resources required to start and run your business to determine whether it's feasible.

4.3.5. Legal and regulatory considerations: What legal and regulatory requirements will you need to comply with? You need to understand the legal and regulatory landscape to ensure that your business is compliant and avoid any legal issues.

By carefully evaluating online business opportunities, entrepreneurs can determine whether their business idea is viable and has the potential to succeed. It's important to conduct thorough research and analysis to make informed decisions and increase the likelihood of success.

4.4   Developing a business plan

Developing a business plan is a critical step in starting an online business. It is a written document that outlines the objectives, strategies, and tactics for achieving success. A well-crafted business plan serves as a roadmap that guides entrepreneurs through the process of starting and growing their business. Here are some key components of a business plan:

4.4.1. Executive summary: This section provides an overview of the business and its goals. It should be concise, clear, and compelling to grab the reader's attention.

4.4.2. Market analysis: This section evaluates the market demand and competition. It should include information on the target audience, market trends, and competitors.

4.4.3. Business model: This section explains how the business will generate revenue and make a profit. It should include information on pricing, distribution, and marketing strategies.

4.4.4. Operations plan: This section outlines the day-to-day operations of the business, including the processes, systems, and technologies required to run the business.

4.4.5. Financial plan: This section includes financial projections, such as revenue, expenses, and cash flow. It should also include details on funding sources and investment requirements.

Developing a business plan can help entrepreneurs identify potential challenges and opportunities, and develop strategies to overcome them. It can also help secure funding from investors and lenders. A well-written business plan can serve as a powerful tool for achieving success in the highly competitive world of online business.

4.5   *Setting up an online business*

Setting up an online business requires careful planning and execution to ensure its success. Here are some key steps to follow when starting an online business:

4.5.1. Choose a niche: Select a profitable niche that you are passionate about and have expertise in. Research the market demand, competition, and profitability of the niche.

4.5.2. Develop a business plan: Develop a comprehensive business plan that outlines the objectives, strategies, and tactics for achieving success. The plan should include a market analysis, business model, operations plan, and financial plan.

4.5.3. Choose a business name and register it: Choose a memorable and unique business name and register it with the appropriate authorities. Consider trademarking the name to protect your brand.

4.5.4. Build a website: Build a professional website that reflects your brand and offers a seamless user experience. Choose a domain name, hosting platform, and content management system.

4.5.5. Develop a marketing strategy: Develop a comprehensive marketing strategy that includes social media marketing, email marketing, SEO, PPC advertising, and content marketing.

4.5.6. Set up payment and shipping methods: Set up secure and convenient payment methods and shipping options for customers.

4.5.7. Launch the business: Launch the business and promote it through various channels. Continuously evaluate and adjust the business strategy based on customer feedback and market trends.

By following these steps, entrepreneurs can set up a successful online business that generates profits and grows over time. It is important to stay focused, determined, and flexible in the face of challenges and opportunities.

5. MARKETING AN ONLINE BUSINESS

Marketing an online business is a crucial aspect of its success. Without effective marketing, an online business may struggle to attract and retain customers, resulting in low sales and revenue. Marketing an online business involves promoting its products or services to a targeted audience using various online marketing channels such as social media, email marketing, SEO, PPC advertising, and content marketing. Effective marketing helps to increase brand awareness, generate leads, and drive conversions. In this section, we will explore the different marketing strategies and tactics that can be used to promote and grow an online business.

5.1   Creating a website

Creating a website is a critical component of marketing an online business. A website serves as the primary platform for showcasing products or services, providing information to customers, and facilitating transactions. Here are the key steps involved in creating a website for an online business:

5.1.1. Choose a domain name: A domain name is the web address of the website, and it should be relevant to the business and easy to remember.

5.1.2. Select a hosting provider: A hosting provider is responsible for storing the website files and making them accessible to visitors on the internet. Choose a reliable hosting provider that offers scalable solutions for growing businesses.

5.1.3. Choose a content management system (CMS): A CMS is a software application used to create, manage, and publish digital content on the website. Popular CMS options include WordPress, Wix, and Squarespace.

5.1.4. Design the website: Choose a website template or work with a designer to create a customized website design that reflects the brand and appeals to the target audience.

5.1.5. Add content: Add relevant and engaging content to the website, including product descriptions, blog posts, and customer testimonials.

5.1.6. Optimize for search engines: Optimize the website for search engines by using relevant keywords, creating high-quality content, and building backlinks.

5.1.7. Test and launch: Test the website thoroughly to ensure it is functioning properly and launch it to the public.

By following these steps, businesses can create a professional and effective website that serves as a powerful marketing tool for promoting their products or services and attracting and retaining customers.

5.2   Content marketing

Content marketing is a marketing strategy that focuses on creating and sharing valuable, relevant, and consistent content to attract and retain a clearly defined audience and ultimately drive profitable customer action. Content marketing aims to educate and inform the target audience, rather than overtly promoting products or services.

Content marketing involves creating various types of content, such as blog posts, social media updates, videos, podcasts, infographics, and e-books. The content should be high-quality, relevant, and engaging, and it should provide value to the target audience. The goal is to establish the business as a thought leader and trusted authority in the industry, which can lead to increased brand awareness, website traffic, and ultimately, conversions.

Effective content marketing requires a strategic approach, including identifying the target audience, developing a content plan, and measuring the success of the campaign. Businesses can use various metrics to measure the success of content marketing, such as website traffic, social media engagement, email open rates, and lead conversions.

Content marketing is a cost-effective and powerful way for businesses to reach their target audience, establish brand credibility, and drive profitable customer action. By creating valuable and relevant content that educates and informs the target audience, businesses can build a loyal following and ultimately grow their customer base.

5.3   Social media marketing

Social media marketing refers to the process of using social media platforms such as Facebook, Instagram, Twitter, LinkedIn, and others to promote a business, its products or services, and engage with its target audience.

Social media marketing allows businesses to connect with their target audience on a personal level, build brand awareness, and increase customer loyalty. It involves creating and sharing content that is specifically designed to engage the target audience and drive them to take action, such as visiting a website, making a purchase, or sharing content with others.

There are various types of social media marketing strategies, including paid social media advertising, influencer marketing, and organic social media marketing. Paid social media advertising involves using sponsored posts, ads, and promoted content to reach a larger audience. Influencer marketing involves partnering with social media influencers to promote products or services to their followers. Organic social media marketing involves creating and sharing high-quality, engaging content to attract and retain a following.

Social media marketing requires a strategic approach, including identifying the target audience, developing a social media plan, creating and sharing content, and measuring the success of the campaign. By effectively using social media marketing, businesses can increase their reach and engagement with their target audience, build brand awareness, and ultimately drive profitable customer action.

5.4   *Search engine optimization*

Search engine optimization (SEO) is the practice of optimizing a website to improve its ranking and visibility on search engine results pages (SERPs). The goal of SEO is to increase organic, or non-paid, traffic to a website by making it more visible to search engine users who are searching for specific keywords or phrases related to the business or its products and services.

SEO involves a range of techniques and strategies, including keyword research, on-page optimization, link building, and content creation. Keyword research involves identifying relevant keywords and phrases that potential customers might use when searching for products or services related to the business. On-page optimization involves optimizing the website's content, structure, and HTML code to improve its relevance and ranking for specific keywords.

Link building involves creating high-quality backlinks to the website from other reputable websites, which helps to increase the website's authority and credibility in the eyes of search engines. Content creation involves creating high-quality, engaging, and relevant content that appeals to the website's target audience and encourages them to engage with the website.

SEO is a long-term strategy that requires ongoing monitoring, analysis, and optimization to ensure that the website continues to rank well on SERPs. By effectively implementing SEO strategies, businesses can increase their visibility and reach on search engines, attract more organic traffic, and ultimately drive more leads, conversions, and revenue.

5.5   Email marketing

Email marketing is a digital marketing strategy that involves sending promotional or informative messages to a targeted audience via email. The goal of email marketing is to build relationships with customers, increase brand awareness, and drive sales by encouraging recipients to take action, such as making a purchase or visiting a website.

Email marketing can be used for a variety of purposes, such as promoting a new product or service, announcing a sale or promotion, providing educational content, or nurturing leads. The key to successful email marketing is delivering relevant and valuable content to the right audience at the right time.

To effectively implement an email marketing strategy, businesses must first build an email list of subscribers who have opted in to receive messages. This can be done by offering incentives, such as exclusive content or discounts, in exchange for email addresses.

Once an email list is established, businesses can create and send targeted email campaigns using email marketing software. These campaigns can be personalized based on subscriber data, such as past purchases or interests, to increase engagement and relevance.

Email marketing campaigns should be optimized for deliverability, open rates, and click-through rates. This can be achieved through strategies such as testing subject lines, segmenting email lists, and using clear and concise messaging.

By effectively using email marketing, businesses can increase customer engagement and loyalty, drive traffic and sales, and ultimately grow their business.

5.6   Paid advertising

Paid advertising is a marketing strategy where businesses pay to display their ads to a targeted audience on various platforms such as search engines, social media networks, and other websites. Paid advertising can be an effective way to quickly generate traffic, leads, and sales for a business.

There are various types of paid advertising, such as pay-per-click (PPC) advertising, display advertising, social media advertising, and sponsored content. PPC advertising is the most common type of paid advertising where businesses bid on keywords related to their products or services, and their ads are displayed at the top of search engine results pages when users search for those keywords.

Display advertising, on the other hand, involves placing banner ads on websites related to the business's industry or target audience. Social media advertising involves promoting ads on social media platforms such as Facebook, Instagram, Twitter, and LinkedIn.

Sponsored content is another type of paid advertising where businesses pay to have their content promoted on third-party websites or social media platforms.

To effectively use paid advertising, businesses must first define their target audience and choose the right platform to reach them. They must also set a budget and bid strategically to optimize their ad placement and cost-per-click.

Paid advertising campaigns should also be optimized for ad relevance, click-through rate, and conversion rate. This can be achieved through strategies such as creating compelling ad copy and visuals, targeting specific demographics and interests, and regularly testing and adjusting ad campaigns.

By using paid advertising, businesses can quickly reach their target audience and generate traffic, leads, and sales for their business. However, it's important to use paid advertising in conjunction with other marketing strategies to build a sustainable and effective marketing strategy.

6. SCALING AN ONLINE BUSINESS

Scaling an online business involves expanding the operations of the business to reach a wider audience, generate more revenue, and increase profits. It requires careful planning and execution to ensure that the growth of the business is sustainable and profitable. Scaling can be achieved through a variety of methods, such as launching new products or services, expanding marketing efforts, optimizing business processes, and increasing production capacity. However, scaling a business can also bring new challenges, such as managing increased demand, maintaining quality standards, and ensuring adequate resources and infrastructure to support growth. Therefore, it is important to have a clear strategy and plan in place before scaling a business to avoid any potential pitfalls.

6.1 Hiring freelancers and employees

Hiring freelancers and employees is a crucial part of scaling an online business. Freelancers and employees can help business owners to manage increasing demand, expand their operations, and free up time to focus on core business functions. However, there are important differences between hiring freelancers and employees, and it is important to understand these differences before making any hiring decisions.

Freelancers are typically hired on a project-by-project basis, and they work independently, often from remote locations. They are responsible for their own taxes, insurance, and other expenses. Freelancers offer flexibility and cost-effectiveness, as they can be hired for short-term projects without the need for long-term commitments.

Employees, on the other hand, work directly for the business and are typically paid a salary or hourly wage. They are subject to tax withholding, benefits, and other employment regulations. Employees offer consistency and reliability, as they can be trained and managed to ensure that they meet the needs of the business.

When deciding whether to hire freelancers or employees, it is important to consider the specific needs of the business. Freelancers may be suitable for short-term projects or for filling skills gaps that cannot be easily filled by existing staff. Employees may be more appropriate for longer-term roles, such as customer service or administrative positions.

Regardless of whether the business owner chooses to hire freelancers or employees, it is important to establish clear hiring criteria, provide proper training and support, and maintain clear lines of communication to ensure that everyone is working towards the same goals.

6.2   *Automating processes*

Automating processes refers to the use of technology and tools to streamline and simplify repetitive tasks and processes in an online business. This can range from automating email marketing campaigns to setting up chatbots to handle customer inquiries. By automating processes, businesses can save time, reduce errors, and increase efficiency, allowing them to focus on growing and expanding their business.

There are many tools and platforms available for businesses to automate their processes, including customer relationship management (CRM) software, email marketing platforms, social media scheduling tools, and project management software. For example, a business can use a CRM software to automatically send follow-up emails to leads or customers, or use social media scheduling tools to automate the posting of content on social media platforms.

However, it is important for businesses to strike a balance between automation and personalization. While automation can save time and increase efficiency, it is important to maintain a personal touch with customers and clients. Therefore, businesses should ensure that they are using automation in a way that complements their overall strategy and does not sacrifice the human connection with their audience.

6.3   *Expanding product and service offerings*

Expanding product and service offerings is an important step for online businesses looking to scale and grow. This involves introducing new products or services to existing customers or targeting new markets to increase revenue and reach.

One way to expand product and service offerings is to conduct market research to identify potential gaps in the market or untapped customer needs. This can involve surveying existing customers or analyzing data on industry trends and consumer behavior.

Once potential products or services have been identified, businesses should develop a strategy for launching and promoting them. This can involve creating a marketing plan, setting pricing and sales targets, and establishing partnerships or collaborations to increase exposure and reach.

Another approach to expanding product and service offerings is to diversify revenue streams. This can involve offering complementary products or services, creating subscription-based models, or launching digital products such as e-books or online courses.

However, it is important for businesses to approach product and service expansion strategically and carefully. Expanding too quickly or without sufficient research can lead to oversaturation or a loss of focus. Therefore, businesses should carefully consider their resources, capabilities, and long-term goals before embarking on any expansion efforts.

6.4   *Entering new markets*

Entering new markets is a crucial step in the growth and expansion of an online business. It involves identifying potential new markets and determining the feasibility of entering them. This process involves research and analysis of market trends, consumer behavior, competition, and regulatory requirements.

One way to enter a new market is to expand the product or service offerings to cater to the specific needs of the target market. This may require customization or localization of the existing offerings to align with the cultural and linguistic differences in the new market. Another way to enter a new market is to establish partnerships or collaborations with local businesses or individuals who have an established presence and network in the target market. This can help in building brand awareness and credibility in the new market.

Before entering a new market, it is important to conduct a thorough market research to evaluate the potential risks and benefits associated with the expansion. The research should include analysis of the competitive landscape, regulatory requirements, cultural nuances, and consumer behavior. Based on the findings, a strategic plan can be developed to ensure a successful entry into the new market. The plan should include clear objectives, timelines, budget, and performance metrics to measure the success of the expansion.

In conclusion, entering new markets is a critical step in the growth and expansion of an online business. It requires careful planning, research, and execution to ensure success in the new market. By expanding product and service offerings, establishing partnerships, and conducting thorough market research, an online business can successfully enter new markets and grow its customer base.

6.5   *Leveraging partnerships and collaborations*

Partnerships and collaborations can be valuable strategies for scaling an online business. By working with other businesses or individuals, you can leverage their audience, expertise, and resources to expand your reach and offerings.

There are several ways to form partnerships and collaborations in the online business world. Here are a few examples:

6.5.1. Affiliate marketing: This involves partnering with other businesses or individuals who promote your products or services in exchange for a commission on any resulting sales.

6.5.2. Joint ventures: A joint venture is a partnership between two or more businesses or individuals to jointly develop and market a product or service. This can be an effective way to share resources and expertise, as well as risks and rewards.

6.5.3. Co-creation: This involves collaborating with customers or other businesses to develop new products or services that meet their needs. By involving customers or partners in the development process, you can create offerings that are more likely to succeed in the market.

6.5.4. Cross-promotion: This involves partnering with other businesses or individuals to promote each other's products or services. By sharing audiences and resources, you can reach new customers and build brand awareness.

When entering into partnerships and collaborations, it's important to choose partners that align with your values and goals, and to establish clear expectations and communication channels. With the right partners and strategies in place, partnerships and collaborations can be powerful tools for scaling your online business.

6.6   *Diversifying income streams*

Diversifying income streams refers to the practice of generating income from multiple sources, instead of relying on a single source. This is an important strategy for individuals and businesses alike, as it helps to mitigate risks and ensure financial stability. By diversifying income streams, one can create a more sustainable and resilient financial foundation.

One common example of diversifying income streams is investing in multiple stocks or mutual funds, instead of relying on a single company's stock for all of one's investment returns. Another example is creating multiple streams of passive income, such as rental properties, affiliate marketing, or royalties from intellectual property.

In the context of an online business, diversifying income streams may involve expanding product or service offerings, entering new markets, and leveraging partnerships and collaborations. It may also involve developing new revenue streams, such as online courses, membership programs, or consulting services.

Overall, diversifying income streams can provide a number of benefits, including increased financial security, greater flexibility, and more opportunities   for   growth   and   innovation.

7. LEGAL AND FINANCIAL CONSIDERATIONS

Starting an online business requires attention to legal and financial considerations, just like any other business. These considerations ensure that the business operates within legal boundaries and has sound financial management. Failing to address these concerns can lead to legal issues, financial losses, and potential damage to the business's reputation.

One crucial legal consideration is to register the business and obtain any necessary licenses and permits. The legal structure of the business, such as sole proprietorship, LLC, or corporation, also needs to be determined. Each structure has its advantages and disadvantages in terms of taxes, liability, and compliance requirements. It is important to consult with a legal professional to choose the right structure for the business.

Financial considerations include creating a budget, setting up a bookkeeping system, and obtaining business insurance. A budget outlines the business's income and expenses and helps to plan for future growth. A bookkeeping system tracks income and expenses, generates financial reports, and helps to manage cash flow. Business insurance protects against unexpected events, such as accidents or liability claims, that can harm the business financially.

Lastly, online businesses need to comply with data privacy and security regulations. Personal information collected from customers' needs to be protected and managed securely. The business should have policies and procedures in place to safeguard customer data and prevent breaches.

In conclusion, online businesses need to pay attention to legal and financial considerations to ensure compliance and financial stability. Seeking professional advice and developing systems and policies can help to avoid costly mistakes and protect the business's reputation.

7.1 Business registration and taxes

When starting an online business, it is essential to consider the legal and financial aspects of the business. One of the first steps is to register the business with the appropriate authorities in the jurisdiction where the business operates. This could involve registering a business name, obtaining a business license, and setting up tax accounts with the relevant authorities. The tax laws and regulations vary depending on the jurisdiction, and it is crucial to seek professional advice to ensure compliance. The business structure also impacts the tax implications, and the entrepreneur must decide on the most appropriate structure for their business.

Some popular business structures include sole proprietorship, partnership, limited liability company (LLC), and corporation. Each has its advantages and disadvantages, and it is essential to understand the legal and tax implications of each before making a decision. Additionally, the business owner must maintain proper financial records and ensure that they separate their personal finances from their business finances. This helps to ensure that they can track business expenses and income accurately and report their taxes correctly.

7.2 Contracts and agreements

Contracts and agreements are legal documents that define the terms and conditions of a business transaction between two or more parties. These documents are essential in any business transaction as they help to establish clear expectations and prevent misunderstandings or disputes. Contracts can be used in a variety of situations, such as hiring freelancers or employees, renting office space, or purchasing goods or services.

When creating a contract, it is important to include the following elements:

i. Identification of the parties involved

ii. Description of the goods or services to be provided

iii. Payment terms and conditions

iv. Delivery or completion dates

v. Warranties and guarantees

vi. Confidentiality and non-disclosure agreements

vii. Termination or cancellation clauses

viii. Governing law and jurisdiction

Agreements, on the other hand, are generally less formal than contracts and may not be legally binding. However, they can still be useful in establishing a clear understanding between parties. For example, an agreement could be used to outline the terms of a collaboration or partnership.

It is important to consult with a legal professional when creating contracts and agreements to ensure that they are legally sound and enforceable.

7.3   Financial management

Financial management is a crucial aspect of running a successful online business. It involves monitoring and analyzing the financial performance of the business, as well as making informed decisions based on financial data. This can include budgeting, forecasting, cash flow management, and financial reporting. As an online business owner, it is important to have a clear understanding of your business finances and to stay organized in your financial management practices.

One key aspect of financial management for online businesses is keeping track of expenses and revenue. This can be done through accounting software, spreadsheets, or other financial tracking tools. It is also important to maintain accurate records of transactions, invoices, and receipts to ensure that all expenses and revenue are accounted for and properly categorized.

Another important consideration in financial management is cash flow management. Online businesses often have unique cash flow patterns, and it is important to be aware of fluctuations in revenue and expenses. This can help you make informed decisions about budgeting and spending, and can also help you plan for growth and expansion.

In addition to monitoring and managing finances, online business owners also need to be aware of legal and regulatory requirements related to financial management. This can include tax laws, accounting standards, and other financial regulations that may apply to your business. By staying up-to-date on these requirements, you can avoid potential legal and financial issues and ensure that your business is in compliance with all relevant regulations.

7.4   *Protecting intellectual property*

Protecting your intellectual property is crucial when running an online business. This includes trademarks, copyrights, and patents. By protecting your intellectual property, you can prevent others from using your ideas or products without your permission, and it can also help establish your brand's unique identity. It's essential to consult with a lawyer to ensure that all of your intellectual property is protected properly. In addition, you may want to consider registering your trademarks and patents to prevent others from using them without your permission.

Here is a detailed list of points on protecting intellectual property in the context of online business:

7.4.1. Understand your intellectual property (IP) rights: Intellectual property includes trademarks, patents, copyrights, trade secrets, and more. Before you start your online business, it's important to research and understand the different types of IP protections available and determine which ones apply to your business.

7.4.2. Register your trademarks and patents: If you have a unique business name, logo, or product, you should consider registering for trademarks and patents. This will help protect your brand and prevent others from using or copying your ideas.

7.4.3. Copyright your content: Copyright protection covers creative works such as writing, artwork, music, and videos. By registering your content with the appropriate copyright authorities, you can prevent others from using or profiting from your creations without your permission.

7.4.4. Use contracts and nondisclosure agreements (NDAs): When working with clients, partners, or employees, it's important to have contracts and NDAs in place that protect your intellectual property. These documents can help prevent others from sharing or stealing your ideas or confidential information.

7.4.5. Monitor for infringement: Keep an eye out for potential infringement of your intellectual property rights. This can include monitoring websites and social media accounts for unauthorized use of your content or trademark.

7.4.6. Take action against infringement: If you find that your intellectual property has been infringed upon, you should take immediate action to protect your rights. This can include sending a cease-and-desist letter, filing a lawsuit, or pursuing other legal remedies.

7.4.7. Stay up-to-date with IP laws: Intellectual property laws are constantly evolving, so it's important to stay informed and up-to-date with any changes that may affect your business. This can help you proactively protect your intellectual property rights and avoid potential legal issues.

7.5   Compliance with online regulations

Compliance with online regulations is an essential consideration for any online business. This involves understanding and adhering to various laws and regulations that apply to the online world, such as data protection laws, consumer protection laws, and regulations around online marketing and advertising. Failure to comply with these regulations can result in fines, legal action, and damage to your reputation.

Here are some key points to consider when it comes to compliance with online regulations:

7.5.1. Data protection laws: Online businesses must comply with data protection laws such as the General Data Protection Regulation (GDPR) in the EU and the California Consumer Privacy Act (CCPA) in the US. This includes obtaining consent from individuals to collect their personal data, ensuring that data is stored securely, and providing individuals with access to their data.

7.5.2. Consumer protection laws: Online businesses must comply with consumer protection laws that apply in their jurisdiction. These laws govern issues such as advertising, refunds, and consumer rights. For example, the Federal Trade Commission (FTC) in the US requires businesses to disclose any material connections with endorsers and to avoid making false or misleading claims in advertising.

7.5.3. Online marketing and advertising: Online businesses must comply with regulations around online marketing and advertising, such as the CAN-SPAM Act in the US and the ePrivacy Directive in the EU. This includes obtaining consent for marketing emails, providing an opt-out mechanism, and ensuring that advertising is not misleading or deceptive.

7.5.4. Intellectual property: Online businesses must take steps to protect their own intellectual property, such as trademarks and copyrights, and avoid infringing on the intellectual property of others.

7.5.5. Jurisdictional issues: Online businesses may be subject to regulations in multiple jurisdictions, depending on where their customers are located. It is important to understand the regulations that apply in each jurisdiction and to ensure compliance with each one.

By understanding and complying with online regulations, online businesses can protect themselves from legal and reputational risks and build trust with their   customers.

8. MANAGING CHALLENGES AND RISKS

Managing challenges and risks is a crucial aspect of running any business, and online businesses are no exception. There are various challenges and risks that can arise when operating an online business, including technical difficulties, cyber-attacks, changing market conditions, and legal and regulatory issues. To effectively manage these challenges and risks, it is important to have a solid plan in place and to be proactive in addressing potential issues.

One of the key steps in managing challenges and risks is to stay informed about the latest developments in the industry and to be aware of any changes in regulations or laws that may impact your business. This requires conducting regular research and staying up-to-date with industry news and trends.

Another important aspect of managing challenges and risks is to have contingency plans in place for potential issues. This may include having backup systems and processes in case of technical difficulties, implementing security measures to protect against cyber-attacks, and having a plan for addressing changing market conditions.

It is also essential to have open communication channels with customers and stakeholders, and to be transparent about any issues or challenges that may arise. This can help to build trust and confidence in your business, and can also help to mitigate potential risks.

Finally, it is important to regularly assess and evaluate the effectiveness of your risk management strategies, and to make adjustments as necessary to ensure that your business remains resilient and adaptable to changing conditions. By taking a proactive approach to managing challenges and risks, you can help to ensure the long-term success and sustainability of your online business.

8.1 Common challenges in earning online

Earning online has become an increasingly popular way for individuals to make money and achieve financial freedom. However, like any business or venture, there are several challenges that come with earning online. Here are some common challenges that individuals may face while earning online:

8.1.1. Finding clients: One of the biggest challenges of earning online is finding clients. With so much competition in the online space, it can be difficult to stand out and attract clients to your business.

8.1.2. Building a reputation: Building a strong reputation and brand online takes time and effort. It requires consistently delivering quality work and providing excellent customer service to clients.

8.1.3. Maintaining a steady income: Unlike a traditional job, earning online can be unpredictable, and it can be challenging to maintain a steady income. Freelancers and online business owners must be able to manage their finances and plan accordingly.

8.1.4. Dealing with difficult clients: Working with clients online can sometimes lead to difficult situations. Freelancers and online business owners must be able to handle these situations professionally and effectively.

8.1.5. Managing time effectively: Earning online often requires individuals to work independently and manage their time effectively. Without proper time management skills, it can be easy to fall behind on work or miss important deadlines.

8.1.6. Staying up-to-date with technology: The online space is constantly evolving, and it's important to stay up-to-date with the latest technology and tools to remain competitive.

8.1.7. Dealing with online scams and fraud: Earning online can come with the risk of scams and fraud. It's important to be aware of these risks and take steps to protect yourself and your business.

By understanding and preparing for these challenges, individuals can increase their chances of success while earning online.

8.2   Managing cash flow

Managing cash flow is a critical aspect of running any business, including online businesses. Cash flow refers to the movement of money into and out of a business. In other words, it's the money that comes in and goes out of a business. Proper cash flow management is essential to ensure that there is enough money to pay for expenses such as salaries, bills, and taxes, and to invest in the growth of the business.

Here are some key points to consider when managing cash flow for an online business:

8.2.1. Monitor and forecast cash flow regularly: It's essential to monitor cash flow regularly to ensure that there is enough money to meet ongoing expenses and investments. Regularly forecasting cash flow can also help you identify potential issues before they become problems.

8.2.2. Manage expenses: One way to manage cash flow is to reduce unnecessary expenses. Look for ways to cut costs without compromising the quality of your products or services.

8.2.3. Invoice promptly: Invoicing promptly can help ensure that you receive payment for your products or services as soon as possible. Late payments can cause cash flow problems and make it challenging to manage expenses.

8.2.4. Offer flexible payment options: Offering flexible payment options, such as payment plans, can help make it easier for customers to pay for your products or services. This can help improve cash flow by ensuring that you receive payment for your products or services in a timely manner.

8.2.5. Consider financing options: If you need to invest in the growth of your business, you may want to consider financing options, such as loans or lines of credit. However, it's essential to ensure that you can repay the debt and that it won't negatively impact your cash flow in the long term.

8.2.6. Plan for seasonal fluctuations: If your online business experiences seasonal fluctuations in sales, it's important to plan accordingly. You may need to adjust your expenses, staffing levels, or inventory to ensure that you have enough cash flow to manage the ups and downs of seasonal sales.

8.2.7. Maintain a cash reserve: It's a good idea to maintain a cash reserve to help manage unexpected expenses or cash flow shortages. This reserve can be used to cover expenses or to invest in the growth of your business.

By managing cash flow effectively, online business owners can ensure that their businesses are financially stable and sustainable in the long term.

8.3   Dealing with competition

Dealing with competition is a common challenge faced by online businesses. With the increasing number of online businesses, competition is also growing rapidly. It can be challenging to stand out among competitors and attract customers. To deal with competition, it is important to differentiate your products or services from others. This can be achieved by focusing on your unique selling proposition (USP) and highlighting it in your marketing efforts.

Additionally, keeping an eye on your competitors' strategies and making necessary adjustments in your own business can help you stay ahead of the game. Networking with other business owners in your niche can also provide valuable insights and potential collaboration opportunities. In short, by staying up-to-date with the market trends, continuously improving your offerings, and being open to collaborations, you can effectively manage the challenge of competition in the online business world.

8.4   Handling negative feedback and criticism

As an online business owner, it's important to recognize that negative feedback and criticism are inevitable. However, how you respond to it can greatly impact your reputation and success.

The first step in handling negative feedback and criticism is to listen and acknowledge the concerns of the customer or client. Avoid getting defensive or dismissive, even if you disagree with their comments. Instead, try to understand their perspective and see if there is anything you can do to address their concerns.

It's also important to respond promptly and professionally to negative feedback, whether it's through a public comment or private message. Show that you take their feedback seriously and are committed to resolving any issues.

Another strategy for handling negative feedback and criticism is to use it as an opportunity for improvement. Take the feedback as a chance to learn about areas where your business may be falling short and use it to make changes or improvements to your products or services.

Finally, it's important to have a plan in place for how to handle negative feedback and criticism before it happens. This may involve training your team on how to respond to negative feedback, setting up clear communication channels for customers to provide feedback, and regularly monitoring your online reputation to address any issues promptly. By proactively managing negative feedback and criticism, you can minimize its impact on your business and use it as an opportunity for growth and improvement.

8.5 Mitigating cybersecurity risks

Mitigating cybersecurity risks is an important consideration for any business operating online. Cybersecurity threats can include hacking, data breaches, viruses, malware, and other malicious attacks. To protect against these threats, it is important to take steps such as using secure passwords and two-factor authentication, regularly updating software and systems, and using firewalls and antivirus software.

It is also important to educate employees on cybersecurity best practices and to have a plan in place in case of a security breach. Additionally, businesses can consider hiring a cybersecurity expert or outsourcing security management to a trusted third-party provider. Taking these steps can help mitigate cybersecurity risks and protect the business and its customers from potential harm.

Here are some points on how to mitigate cybersecurity risks:

Implement strong passwords: Use strong, unique passwords and change them frequently. Avoid using the same password for multiple accounts.

Use two-factor authentication: Two-factor authentication adds an extra layer of security to your accounts by requiring a second form of verification.

Keep software up to date: Regularly update your operating system, antivirus software, and other software programs to ensure that they have the latest security updates.

Use firewalls: A firewall can prevent unauthorized access to your computer or network by blocking incoming traffic that may be harmful.

Use encryption: Encryption can help protect your data from cyber-attacks by encoding it in a way that can only be read with a decryption key.

Backup your data: Regularly backup your important data to an external hard drive or cloud storage to ensure that you can recover it if your computer is compromised.

Educate yourself and your team: Educate yourself and your team on the latest cybersecurity threats and how to avoid them, including how to recognize phishing scams and other common tactics used by cybercriminals.

Regularly monitor your systems: Regularly monitor your systems for any suspicious activity, such as unusual login attempts or unauthorized access to your network.

By implementing these measures, you can help mitigate cybersecurity risks and protect your online business from cyber-attacks.

8.6 *Coping with changes in technology and trends*

As technology and trends are constantly evolving, online businesses must adapt and stay up-to-date to remain competitive. Here are some tips for coping with changes in technology and trends:

Stay informed: Keep up-to-date with the latest news and trends in your industry through online publications, social media, and networking events.

Be open to change: Embrace new technologies and trends, and be willing to adapt your business strategy accordingly.

Invest in technology: Invest in the latest tools and software to keep your business running smoothly and efficiently.

Build a strong team: Hire employees and freelancers who are knowledgeable in the latest technology and trends.

Conduct regular assessments: Conduct regular assessments of your business strategy to identify areas that may need updating or improvement.

Engage with your audience: Engage with your audience through social media, online forums, and customer feedback to gain insights into what they want and need from your business.

Continuously improve: Continuously improve your products, services, and customer experience to stay ahead of the competition.

By following these tips, online businesses can stay ahead of the curve and effectively cope with changes in technology and trends.

9. SUCCESS STORIES

ere are some real success stories of individuals who have earned a significant amount of money through online platforms:

Ryan Robinson: Ryan is a content marketing consultant and blogger who has earned over $300,000 in revenue from his blog. He writes about marketing, entrepreneurship, and productivity, and monetizes his blog through affiliate marketing, sponsorships, and digital products. (Source: https://www.ryrob.com/blog-income-report/)

Michelle Schroeder-Gardner: Michelle is a personal finance blogger who has earned over $1 million in revenue from her blog, Making Sense of Cents. She writes about saving money, budgeting, and earning extra income, and monetizes her blog through affiliate marketing, sponsorships, and online courses. (Source: https://www.makingsenseofcents.com/about-me)

Pat Flynn: Pat is an entrepreneur and blogger who has earned over $2 million in revenue from his website, Smart Passive Income. He writes about online business, marketing, and entrepreneurship, and monetizes his blog through affiliate marketing, sponsorships, and online courses. (Source: https://www.smartpassiveincome.com/about/)

Lindsay Ostrom: Lindsay is a food blogger who has earned over $1 million in revenue from her blog, Pinch of Yum. She writes about food, recipes, and photography, and monetizes her blog through affiliate marketing, sponsorships, and digital products. (Source: https://pinchofyum.com/about)

Holly Johnson: Holly is a personal finance blogger who has earned over $2 million in revenue from her blog, Club Thrifty. She writes about saving money, budgeting, and travel, and monetizes her blog through affiliate marketing, sponsorships, and online courses. (Source: https://clubthrifty.com/about-us/)

All of these individuals have achieved significant success through online earning and have built sustainable businesses through their online platforms.

10. CONCLUSION

The world of earning online offers a plethora of opportunities for those seeking financial independence and the ability to work on their own terms. From freelancing to starting a successful online business, the possibilities are endless.

To begin your journey in the online earning world, it is important to identify your strengths, develop a skillset, and create a strong personal brand. Utilizing the right platforms, setting fair prices, and effectively marketing your services are key to attracting and retaining clients.

As you grow your business, it is important to diversify your income streams, continually adapt to changes in technology and trends, and mitigate risks such as cybersecurity threats. By taking the proper legal and financial considerations and surrounding yourself with a strong team, you can turn your online business dreams into a reality.

The online earning world is filled with success stories, from freelancers who have built thriving businesses to entrepreneurs who have transformed small ideas into multi-million dollar ventures. With dedication, hard work, and a willingness to learn and grow, anyone can find success in earning online.

So take the first step today, and begin your journey to financial freedom and a fulfilling career in the online earning world.

10.1 Recap of the book's key points

Throughout this book, we have explored the various aspects of earning money online, from freelancing to starting and scaling an online business. Here are some key points to recap:

i. Freelancing is a popular way to earn money online, and it offers a variety of services like writing, graphic design, programming, and more.

ii. Building a personal brand is crucial for success as a freelancer.

iii. Creating a portfolio is important to showcase your work and attract clients.

iv. Pricing your services correctly is essential to remain competitive in the market.

v. Finding clients is a continuous process and requires a strategic approach.

vi. Online business models like e-commerce, affiliate marketing, and digital products have their own advantages and challenges.

vii. Evaluating online business opportunities is crucial before investing time and money.

viii. Developing a business plan is essential to stay focused and achieve your goals.

ix. Creating a website is vital to establish an online presence and attract customers.

x. Content marketing, social media marketing, SEO, email marketing, and paid advertising are some ways to market an online business.

xi. Scaling an online business involves hiring freelancers and employees, automating processes, expanding product and service offerings, entering new markets, leveraging partnerships and collaborations, and diversifying income streams.

xii. Legal and financial considerations like business registration, taxes, contracts and agreements, financial management, and protecting intellectual property need to be taken care of.

xiii. Managing challenges and risks like cash flow, competition, negative feedback, cybersecurity, and changing technology and trends is necessary to sustain and grow an online business.

These are just some of the key points covered in this book. By implementing the ideas and strategies discussed in this book, you can set yourself up for success in earning money online.

10.2   Final advice for earning online from freelancing to starting a successful online business.

Congratulations on reaching the end of this book on earning online from freelancing to starting a successful online business! As you've learned, the world of online earning is vast and full of opportunities for those who are willing to put in the effort and dedication to succeed.

To summarize some of the key takeaways from this book:

i. Freelancing can be a great way to start earning online, but it's important to establish a strong brand, create a portfolio, set fair prices and rates, and find and retain clients.

ii. Starting an online business requires a solid business plan, a strong online presence including a website, effective marketing strategies, and a plan for scaling and diversifying income streams.

iii. Legal and financial considerations including business registration, taxes, contracts and agreements, and financial management are important to ensure compliance and protect your business.

iv. Common challenges in earning online include managing cash flow, dealing with competition, handling negative feedback and criticism, mitigating cybersecurity risks, and coping with changes in technology and trends.

As you embark on your own online earning journey, keep in mind that success takes time, effort, and persistence. Stay up-to-date with the latest trends and techniques, learn from others, and always be willing to adapt and evolve.

Finally, don't forget that while earning online can provide flexibility and financial freedom, it's important to maintain a work-life balance and prioritize your well-being.

Best of luck on your journey to earning online!

"Rise and Grind"

A Poem on Motivation for Online Earning

Rise and grind, oh ambitious soul,

Online earning is within your goal.

Embrace the challenges that come your way,

And turn them into opportunities to play.

Create a brand that stands apart,

And let it resonate within your heart.

Find your niche, your passion, your dream,

And let your online business take the lead.

With content marketing, SEO and more,

Your online presence will surely soar.

Social media, email marketing, paid ads,

Use them all to reach a wider mass.

But don't forget, amidst the race,

To take a break and find your space.

To rest, to recharge, to rejuvenate,

And come back stronger, more motivated.

Remember, success isn't just about the bucks,

It's about the impact, the joy, the luck.

So keep your purpose at the forefront,

And let your passion drive you to the top.

Rise and grind, oh ambitious soul,

Online earning is within your goal.

Believe in yourself, and let your light shine,

For success will come, one step at a time.

ACKNOWLEDGEMENT

I would like to thank the various online communities and forums that have provided me with valuable insights and information regarding the subject matter of this book. The knowledge and experiences shared by these communities have been instrumental in shaping the content and ideas presented in this book.

Special thanks go to the online platforms and marketplaces that have made earning online possible for millions of people around the world. Your innovative technologies and business models have opened up new avenues for economic growth and opportunity, and have empowered individuals to earn a living on their own terms.

Lastly, I would like to acknowledge the role of technology and artificial intelligence in making the online earning ecosystem possible. In particular, I am grateful for the advancements made by OpenAI and other pioneers in the field, whose breakthroughs in natural language processing, machine learning, and data analytics have revolutionized the way we live and work online.

Without the support and contributions of all these individuals and organizations, this book would not have been possible. Thank you all for your invaluable support and assistance.

ABOUT THE AUTHOR

Malik Shehzad Khan

Malik Shehzad Khan holds a postgraduate degree in Biology. He has a keen interest in both nature and modern technology. This combination of interests suggests that he has a passion for exploring the intersection of these two areas. His background in biology may give him a unique perspective on how technology can be used to better understand and protect the natural world.

www.ingramcontent.com/pod-product-compliance
Lightning Source LLC
Chambersburg PA
CBHW081531220526

45467CB00010B/3136